Sight Words

This book belongs to:

◄ .... ►

CONTENTS:

Sight Word "and" ....Page 1
Sight Word "a" ....Page 2
Sight Word "as" ....Page 3
Sight Word "are" ....Page 4
Sight Word "my" ....Page 5
Sight Word "many" ....Page 6
Sight Word "more" ....Page 7
Sight Word "make" ....Page 8
Sight Word "to" ....Page 9
Sight Word "two" ....Page 10
Sight Word "the" ....Page 11
Sight Word "this" ....Page 12
Sight Word "see" ....Page 13
Sight Word "she" ....Page 14
Sight Word "so" ....Page 15
Sight Word "some" ....Page 16
Sight Word "I" ....Page 17
Sight Word "is" ....Page 18
Sight Word "into" ....Page 19
Sight Word "it" ....Page 20
Sight Word "find" ....Page 21
Sight Word "for" ....Page 22
Sight Word "from" ....Page 23
Sight Word "first" ....Page 24
Sight Word "do" ....Page 25
Sight Word "did" ....Page 26
Sight Word "day" ....Page 27
Sight Word "down" ....Page 28
Sight Word "run" ....Page 29
Sight Word "ride" ....Page 30
Sight Word "on" ....Page 31
Sight Word "of" ....Page 32
Sight Word "out" ....Page 33
Sight Word "over" ....Page 34
Sight Word "go" ....Page 35
Sight Word "get" ....Page 36
Sight Word "good" ....Page 37
Sight Word "green" ....Page 38
Sight Word "like" ....Page 39
Sight Word "look" ....Page 40
Sight Word "long" ....Page 41
Sight Word "little" ....Page 42

Sight Word "he" .... Page 43
Sight Word "here" .... Page 44
Sight Word "have" .... Page 45
Sight Word "how" .... Page 46
Sight Word "use" .... Page 47
Sight Word "up" .... Page 48
Sight Word "can" .... Page 49
Sight Word "come" .... Page 50
Sight Word "call" .... Page 51
Sight Word "could" .... Page 52
Sight Word "be" .... Page 53
Sight Word "big" .... Page 54
Sight Word "before" .... Page 55
Sight Word "by" .... Page 56
Sight Word "no" .... Page 57
Sight Word "now" .... Page 58
Sight Word "not" .... Page 59
Sight Word "number" .... Page 60
Sight Word "each" .... Page 61
Word search .... Page 62
Sight Word "write" .... Page 63
Sight Word "we" .... Page 64
Sight Word "was" .... Page 65
Sight Word "what" .... Page 66
Sight Word "when" .... Page 67
Sight Word "word" .... Page 68
Sight Word "yes" .... Page 69
Sight Word "you" .... Page 70
Sight Word "yellow" .... Page 71
Sight Word "your" .... Page 72
Answer key .... Page 73

and

- Say the word. Then trace the word.

and   and   and

- Write the word.

- Fill in the missing letters to write the word.

a_d   an_   _nd

_ _d   a_ _   _n_

- Complete the sentence with the missing word.

I love my mom ___ dad.

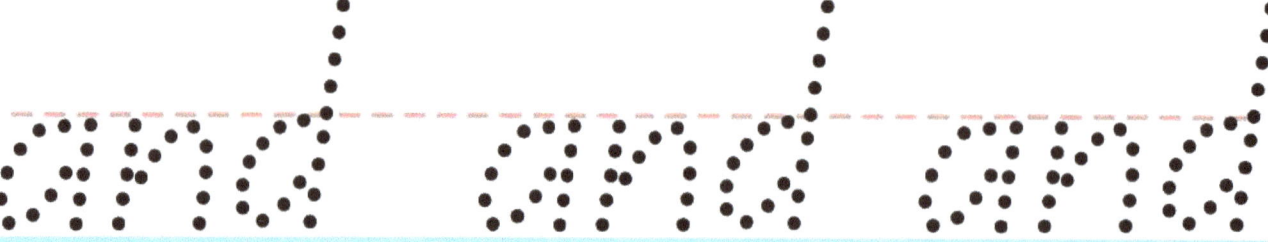

1

- Say the word. Then trace the word.

- Write the word.

- Circle each acorn that has the word **a**.

- Complete the sentence with the missing word.

I see ___ boat.

as

- Say the word. Then trace the word.

⠀⠀⠀⠀as⠀⠀as⠀⠀as⠀⠀as

- Write the word.

- Find and circle the word **as** three times.

a d l k s
s b c x a
s n a s s
c f h i m

- Complete the sentence with the missing word.

Your brother is ___ smart ___ you.

are

- Say the word. Then trace the word.

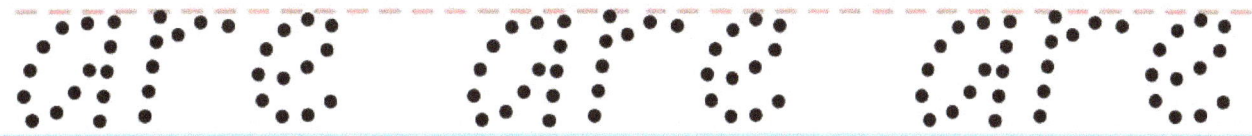

- Write the word.

- Color each space that has the word **are**.

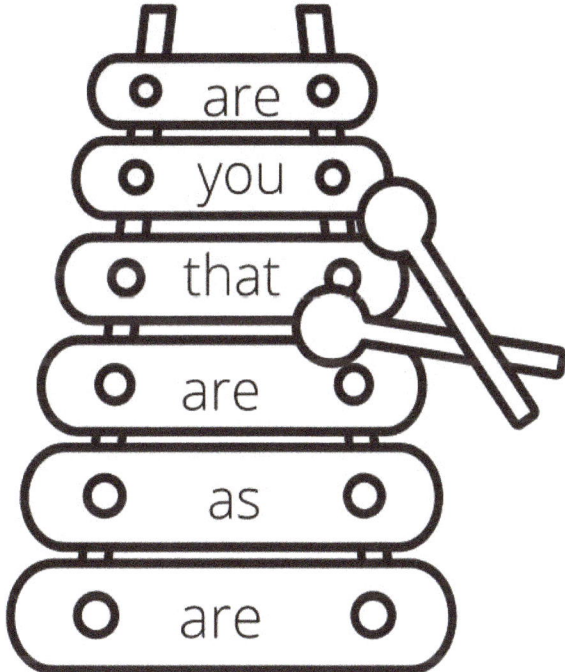

- Complete the sentence with the missing word.

We ___ learning to swim.

my

- Say the word. Then trace the word.

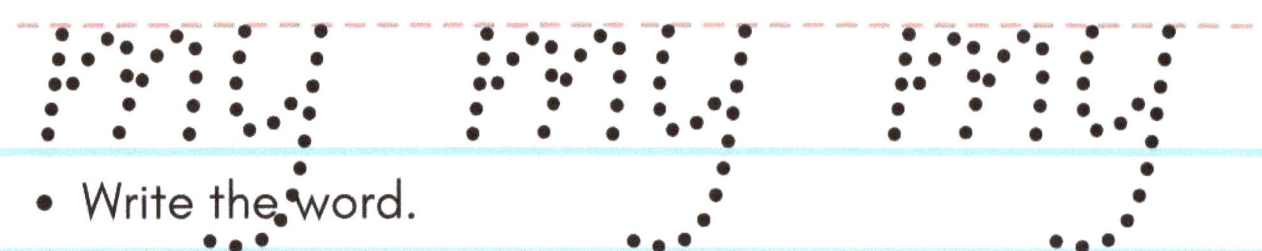

- Write the word.

- Color each space that has the word **my**.

my	by	are	my	a	my
as	my	and	each	my	me
my	more	my	all	my	I

- Complete the sentence with the missing word.

I like ___ dog.

many

- Say the word. Then trace the word.

many   many

- Write the word.

- Fill in the missing letters to write the word.

m__ny   man__

__any

ma__ __   ma__y

- Complete the sentence with the missing word.

I see _____ butterflies.

more

- Say the word. Then trace the word.

more   more

- Write the word.

- Find and circle the word **more** three times.

m d l k s m o r e
o b c x a o d r g
r n a s t r r b a
e f h i m e f m q

- Complete the sentence with the missing word.

I want ___ milk.

make

- Say the word. Then trace the word.

    make   make

- Write the word.

- Circle each apple pie that has the word **make**.

- Complete the sentence with the missing word.

You ___ me smile.

to

- Say the word. Then trace the word. Write the word.

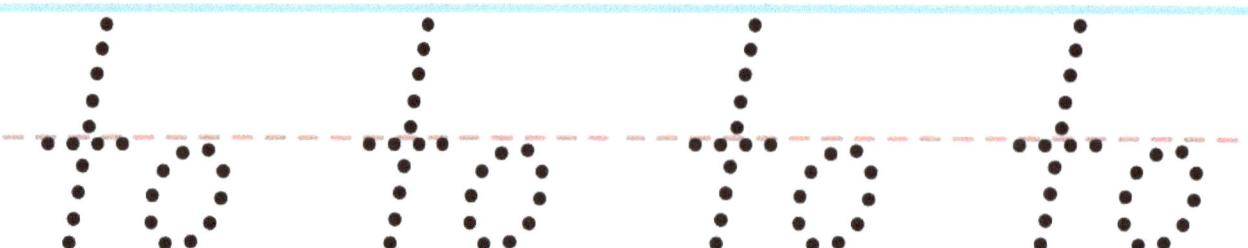

- Color each star that has the word **to**.

- Complete the sentence with the missing word.

I love ___ read.

two

- Say the word. Then trace the word. Write the word.

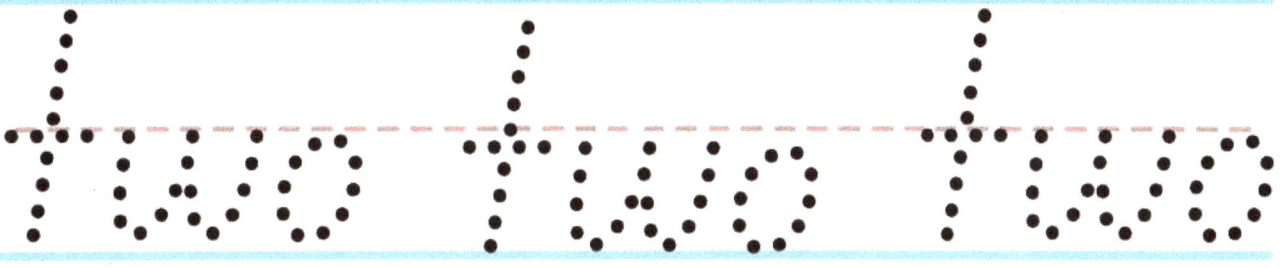

- Find the word **two**. Draw a line to connect the letters.

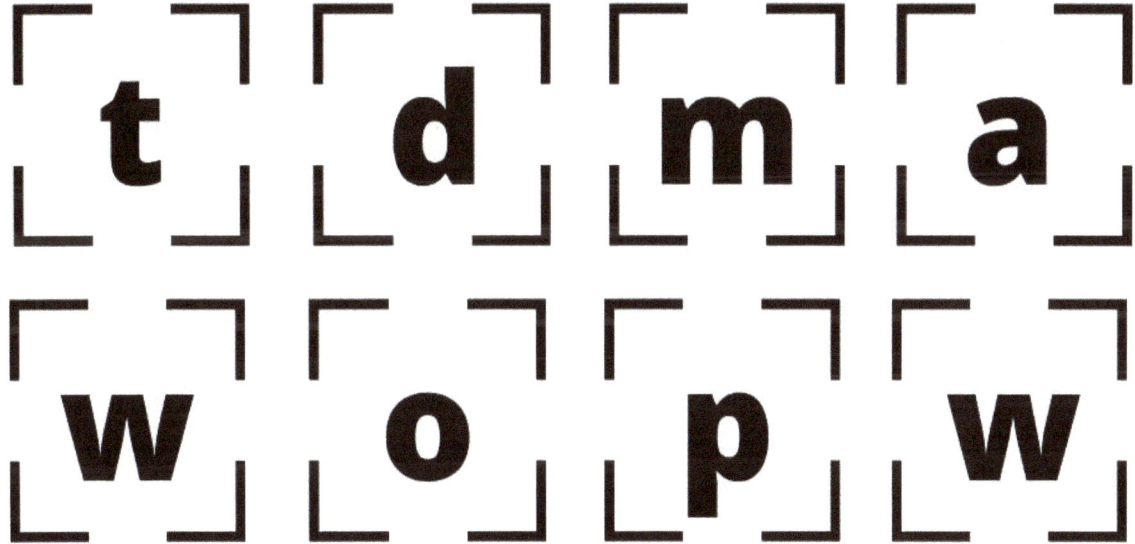

- Complete the sentence with the missing word.

I have ____ hands.

the

- Say the word. Then trace the word. Write the word.

the the the

- Fill in the missing letters to write the word.

t_e   _he   th_

_ _e   _h_   t_ _

- Complete the sentence with the missing word.

_____ apple is red.

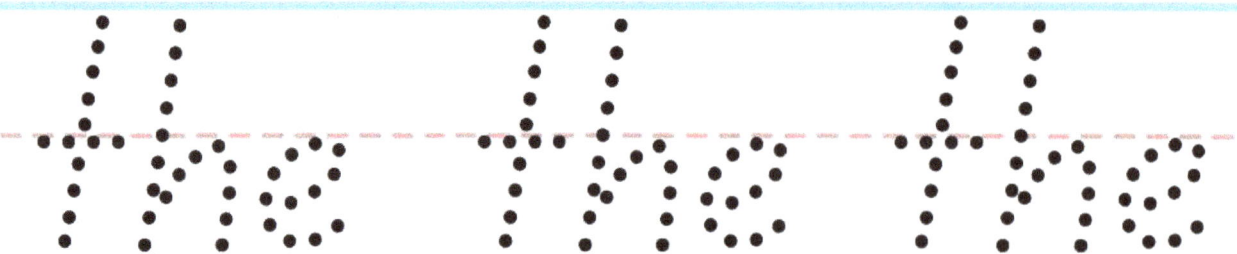

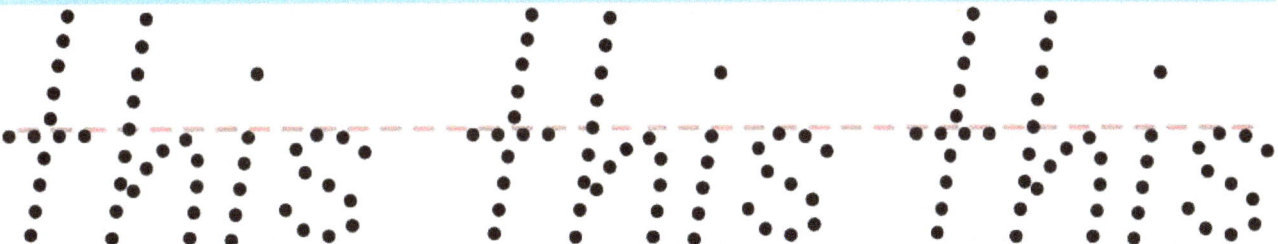

- Say the word. Then trace the word. Write the word.

this this this

- Find and circle the word **this** three times.

t d l k s m o r t
h t h i s o d r h
i n a s t r r b i
s f h i m e f m s

- Complete the sentence with the missing word.

_____ is my cat.

see

- Say the word. Then trace the word. Write the word.

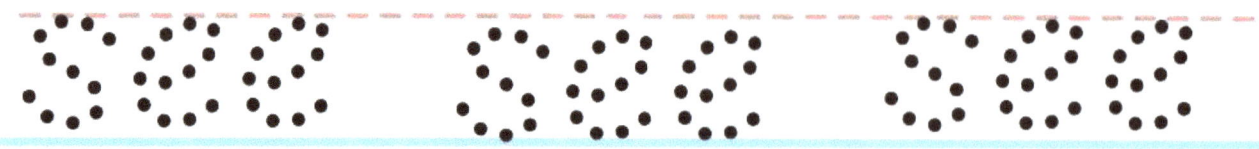

- Color each space that has the word **see**.

- Complete the sentence with the missing word.

I _____ a blue boat.

13

she

- Say the word. Then trace the word. Write the word.

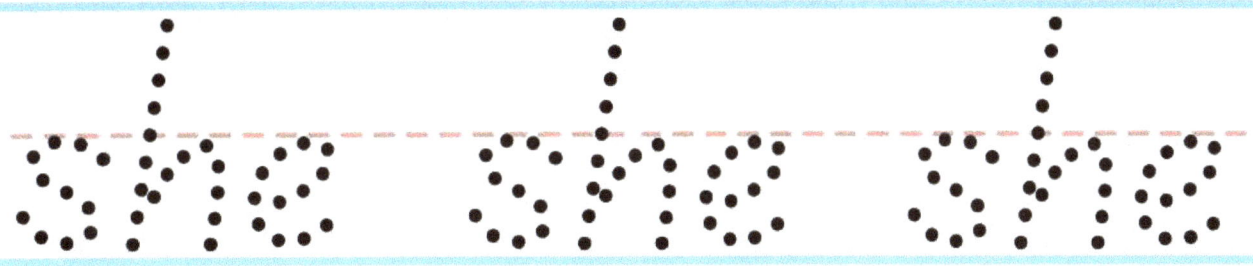

- Find the word **she**. Draw a line to connect the letters.

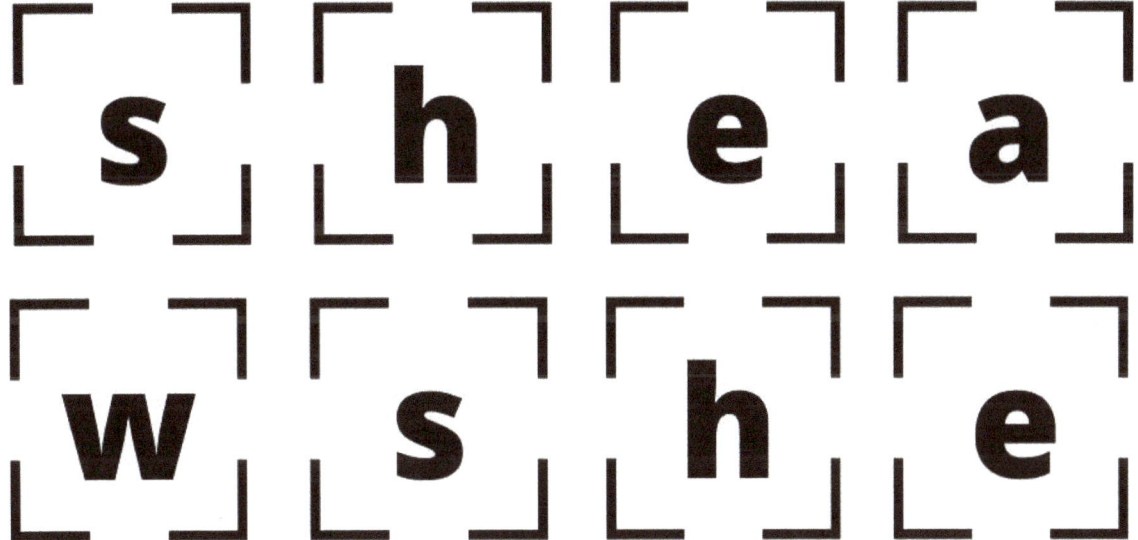

- Complete the sentence with the missing word.

_____ is my sister.

so

- Say the word. Then trace the word. Write the word.

- Circle each fish that has the word **so**.

- Complete the sentence with the missing word.

Ice cream is ____ yummy!

some

- Say the word. Then trace the word. Write the word.

  some   some

- Fill in the missing letters to write the word **some**.

  som_   _ome

  so_ _e   s_ _e

  _o_ _e   s_ _ _

- Complete the sentence with the missing word.

  I want ___ milk.

I

- Say the word. Then trace the word. Write the word.

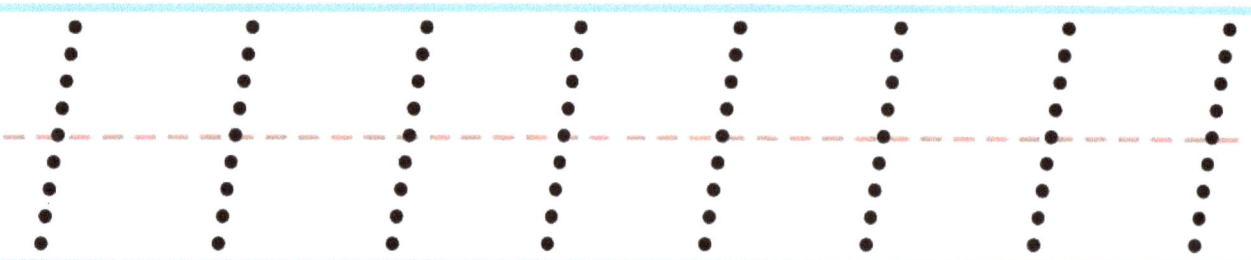

- Color each space that has the word **I**.

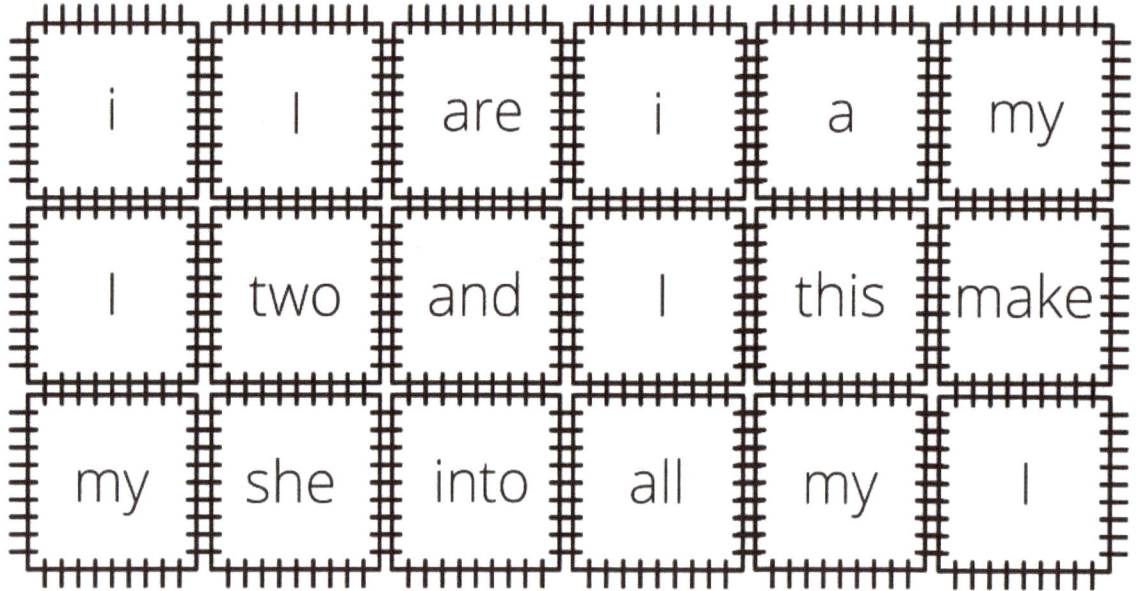

- Complete the sentence with the missing word.

___ **like to write.**

is

- Say the word. Then trace the word. Write the word.

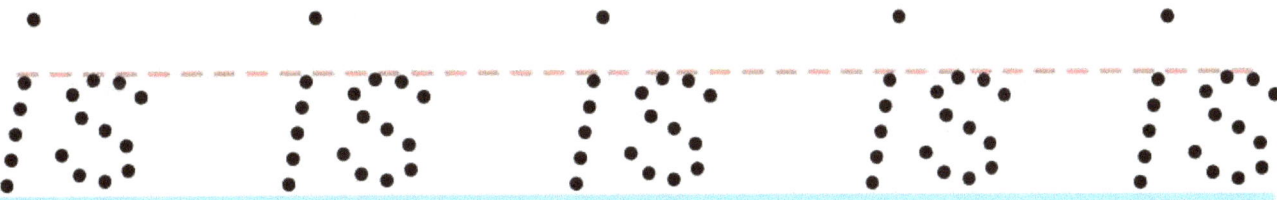

- Color each cloud that has the word **is**.

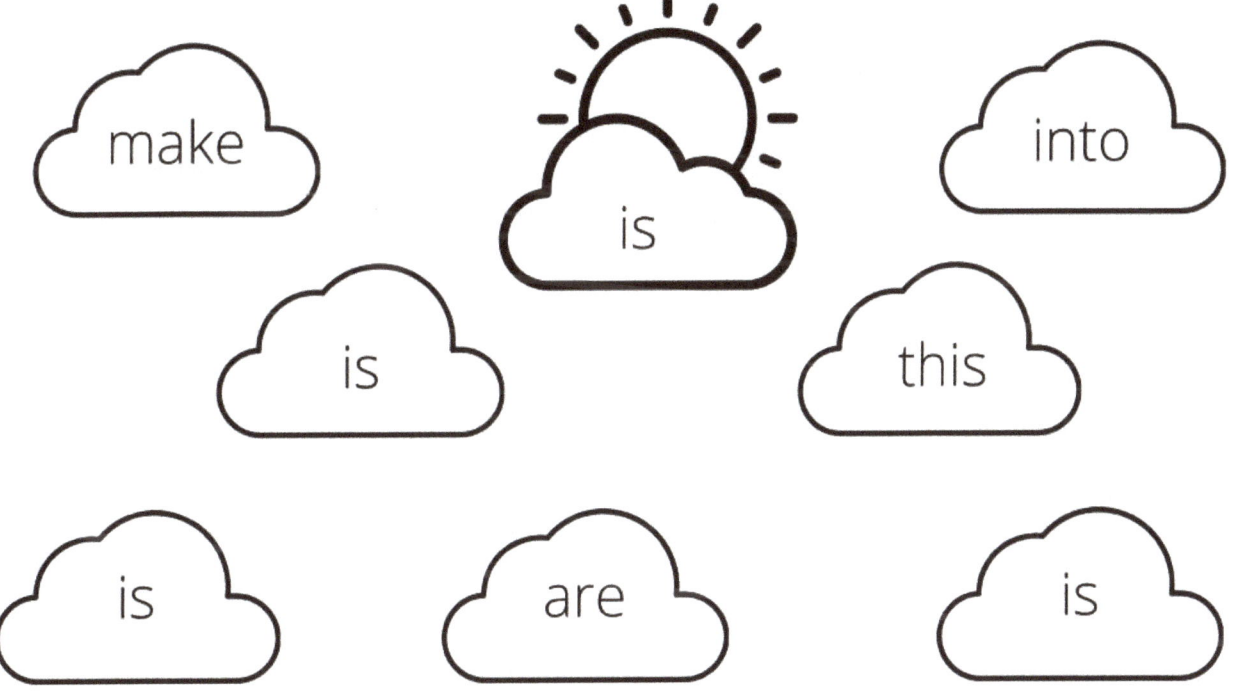

- Complete the sentence with the missing word.

This __ my home.

into

- Say the word. Then trace the word. Write the word.

into into into

- Find the word **into**. Draw a line to connect the letters.

| i | d | t | a |
| w | n | p | o |

- Complete the sentence with the missing word.

Put the toys _____ the box.

19

it

- Say the word. Then trace the word. Write the word.

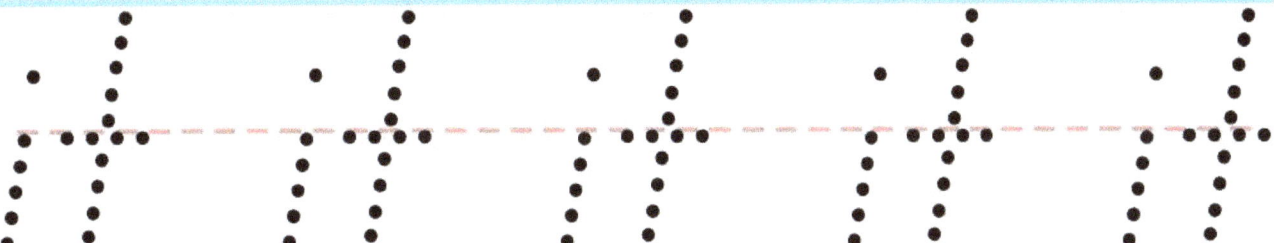

- Circle each hamburger that has the word **it**.

- Complete the sentence with the missing word.

___ is cloudy.

find

- Say the word. Then trace the word. Write the word.

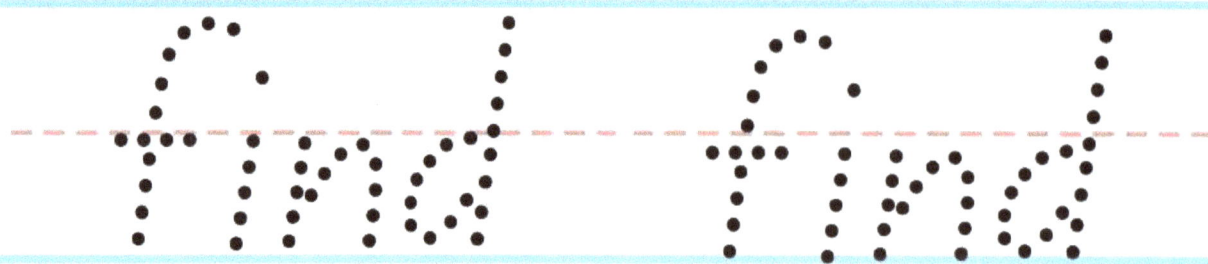

- Color each space that has the word **find**.

i	find	are	find	a	my
find	two	and	this	find	make
my	find	into	find	all	I

- Complete the sentence with the missing word.

I _____ a dog.

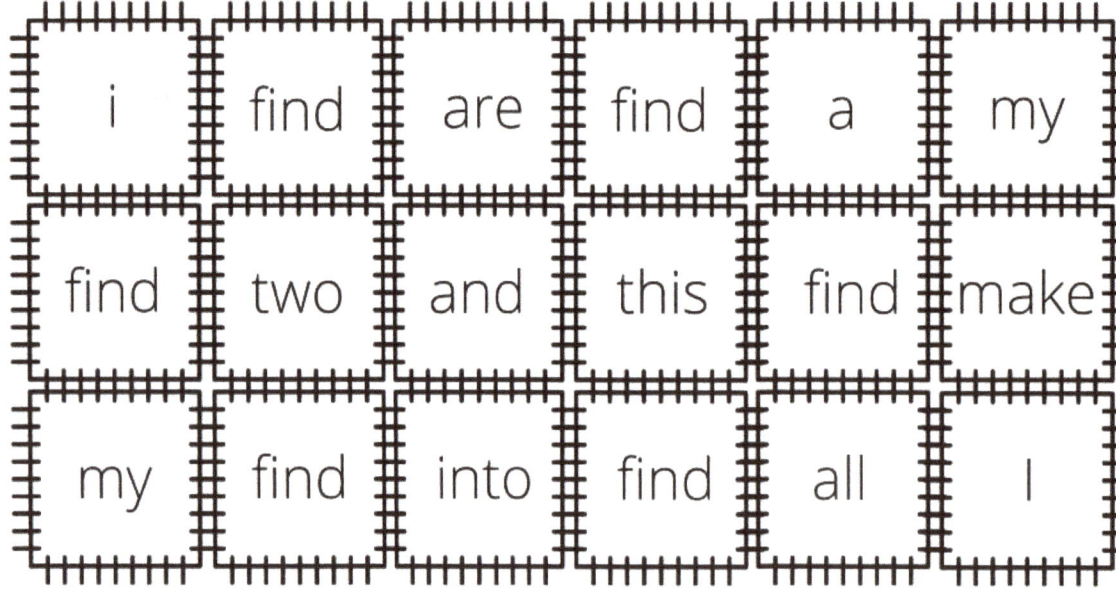

- Say the word. Then trace the word. Write the word.

- Color each tree that has the word **for**.

- Complete the sentence with the missing word.

This is ____ you.

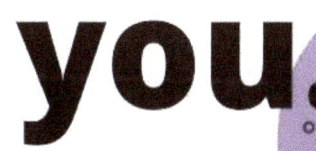

from

- Say the word. Then trace the word. Write the word.

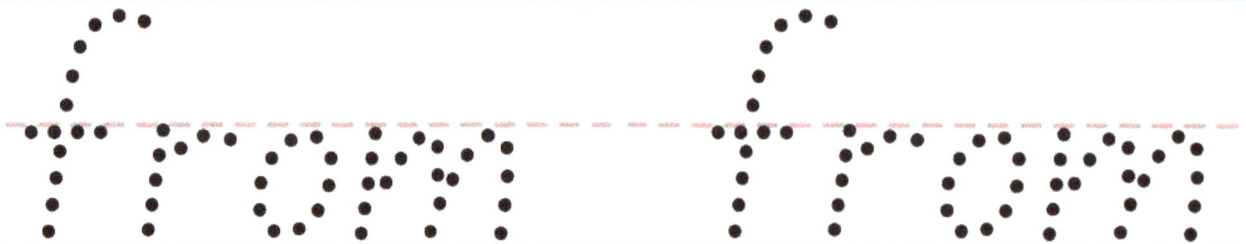

- Fill in the missing letter to write the word **from**.

f_om fr_m fro_

_ _ om f_ _ m

_rom _ _ _m

- Complete the sentence with the missing word.

Where are you _____

23

first

- Say the word. Then trace the word. Write the word.

- Find and circle the word **first** tree times.

f i r s t m o r f
i t h i s o d r i
r n a s t r r b r
s f h i m e f m s
t y h i s o d r t

- Complete the sentence with the missing word.

My _____ name is...

24

do

- Say the word. Then trace the word. Write the word.

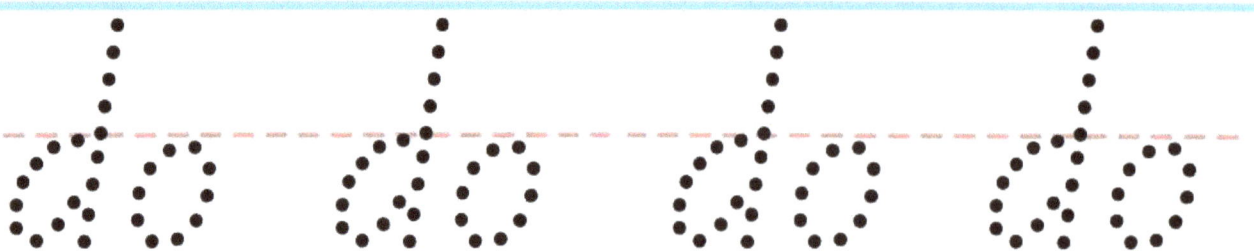

- Color each space that has the word **do**.

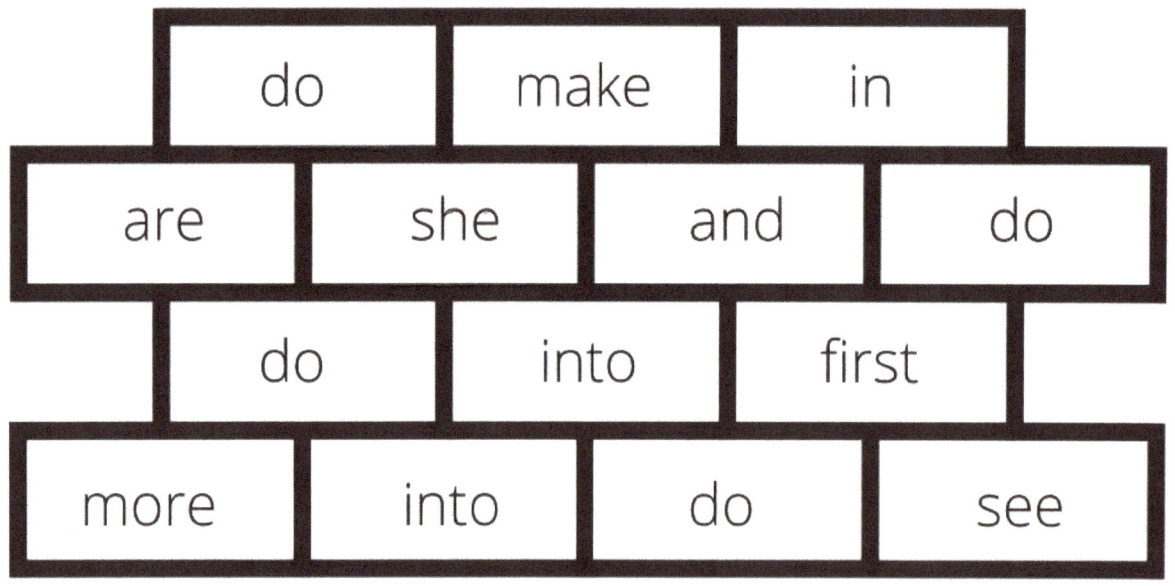

- Complete the sentence with the missing word.

___ you like dogs or cats?

did

- Say the word. Then trace the word. Write the word.

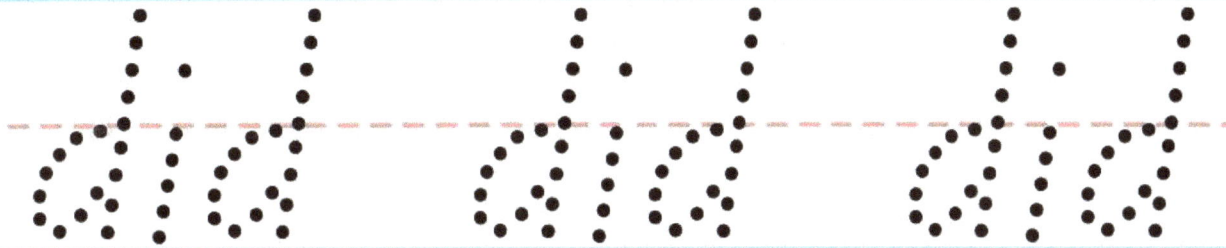

- Find the word **did**. Draw a line to connect the letters.

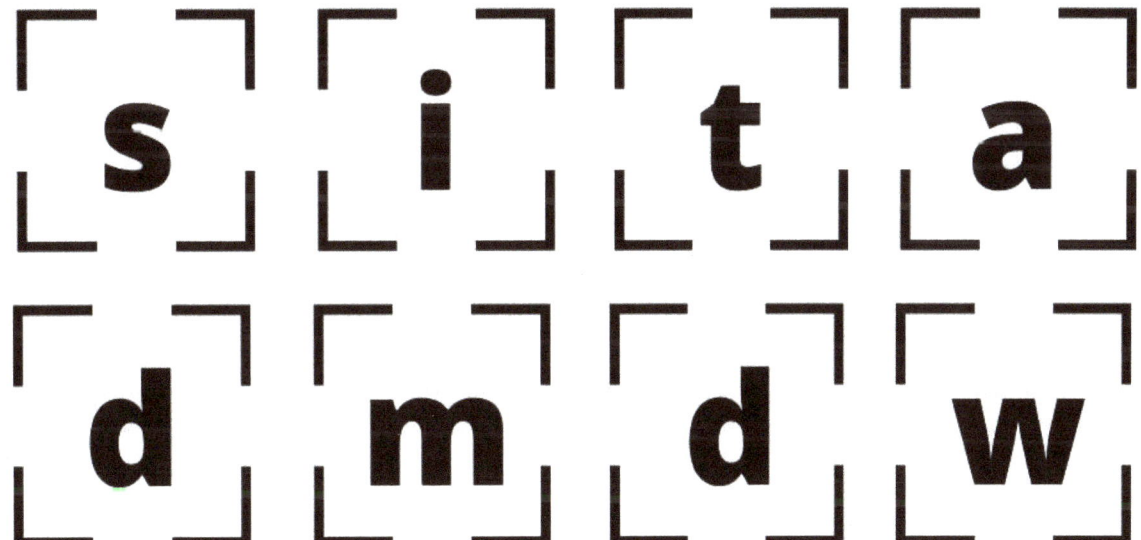

- Complete the sentence with the missing word.

___ you liked the movie?

day

- Say the word. Then trace the word. Write the word.

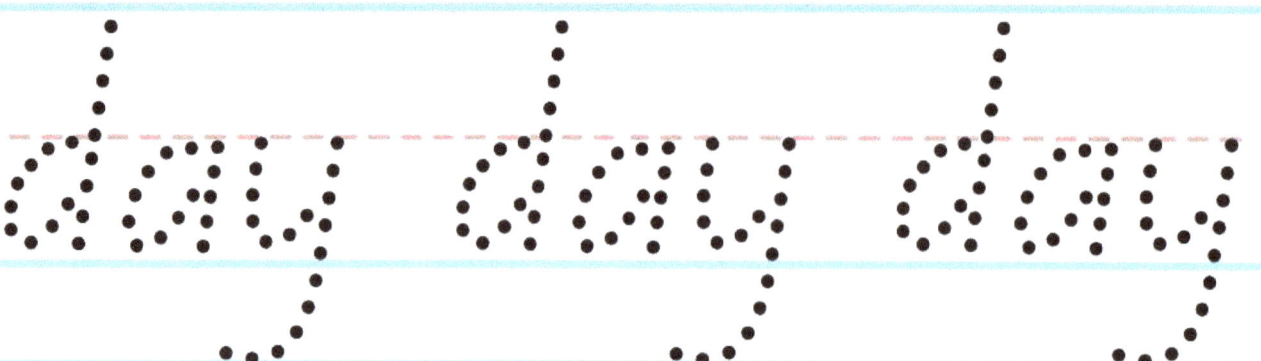

- Circle each image that has the word **day**.

- Complete the sentence with the missing word.

What _____ is today?

down

- Say the word. Then trace the word. Write the word.

  down   down

- Fill in the missing letters to write the word **down**.

  dow_   _own

  do_ _n   d_ _ _n

  _o_ _n   d_ _ _

- Complete the sentence with the missing word.

  Get _____ the table!

run

- Say the word. Then trace the word.

run run run

- Circle each baloon that has the word **run**.

- Complete the sentence with the missing word.

We like to ____.

ride

- Say the word. Then trace the word.

  ride　　ride

- Write the word.

- Fill in the missing letters to write the word.

r_de　_ide　rid_

__de　r_ d_　ri__

___e　_i_ _　r___

- Complete the sentence with the missing word.

I ____ my bike.

on

- Say the word. Then trace the word. Write the word.

- Color each space that has the word **on**.

- Complete the sentence with the missing word.

The mug is ___ the table.

of

- Say the word. Then trace the word. Write the word.

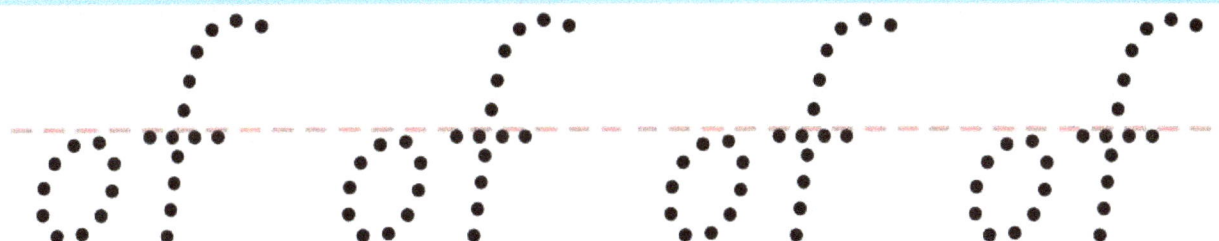

- Find the word **of**. Draw a line to connect the letters.

| o | f | e | m |

| s | o | f | e |

- Complete the sentence with the missing word.

I see a cup ___ tea.

out

- Say the word. Then trace the word. Write the word.

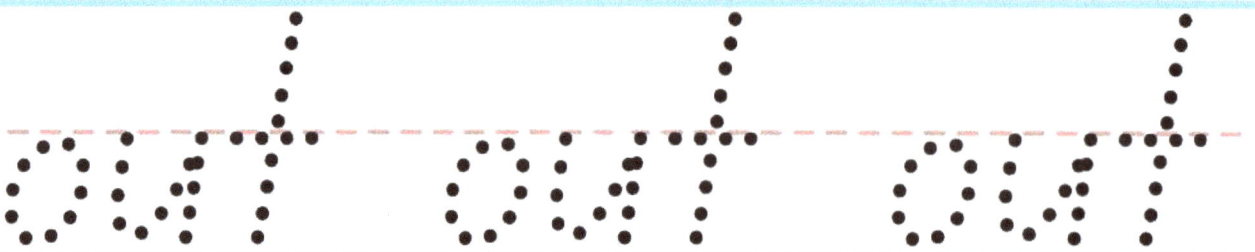

- How many times can you find the word **out**.

- Complete the sentence with the missing word.

Come ___ and play!

over

- Say the word. Then trace the word. Write the word.

over　over

- Fill in the missing letters to write the word **over**.

ove_   _ver

ov_r   o__r

_v_r   o___

- Complete the sentence with the missing word.

The book is ___ there.

34

go

- Say the word. Then trace the word. Write the word.

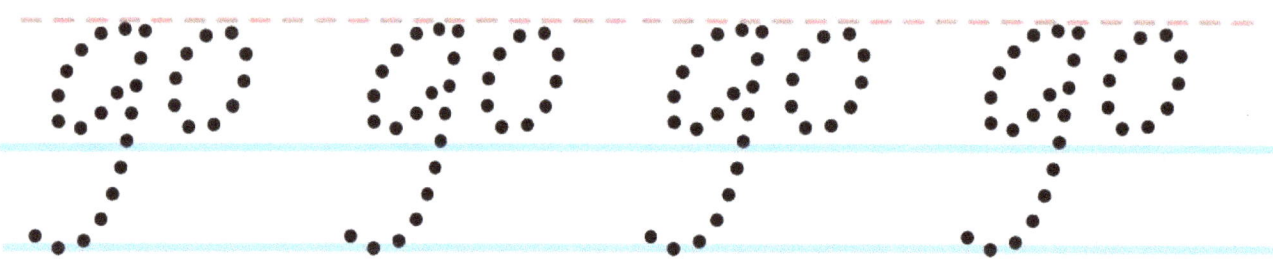

- Color each star that has the word **go**.

- Complete the sentence with the missing word.

I can ___ for a walk.

get

- Say the word. Then trace the word. Write the word.

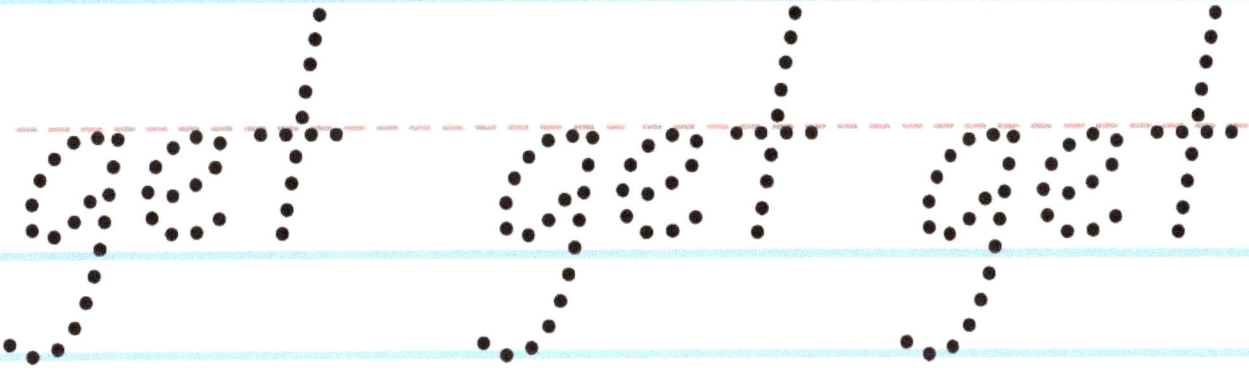

- Find the word **get**. Draw a line to connect the letters.

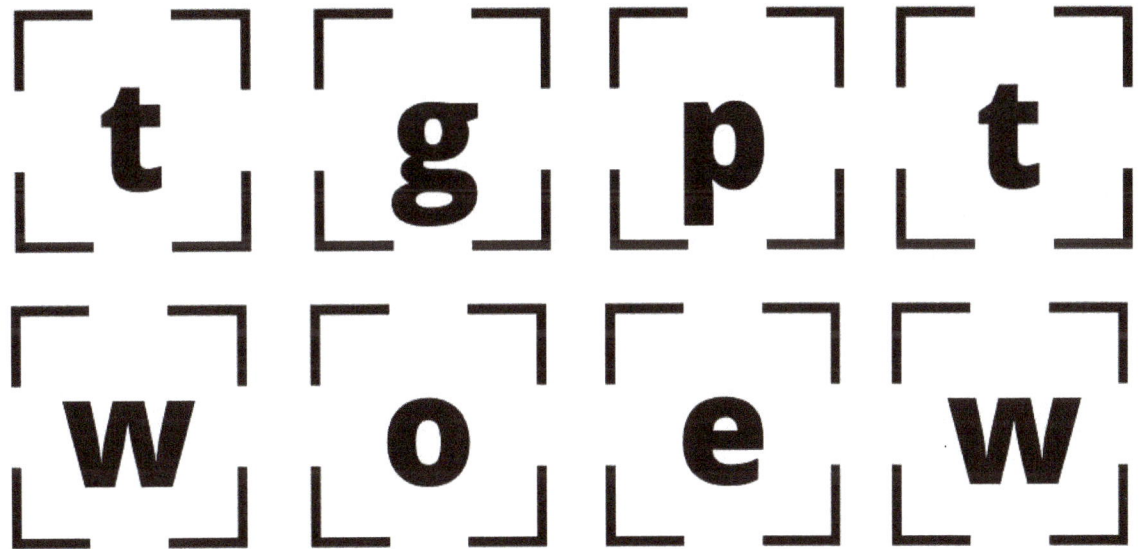

- Complete the sentence with the missing word.

I'll _____ the bill.

good

- Say the word. Then trace the word. Write the word.

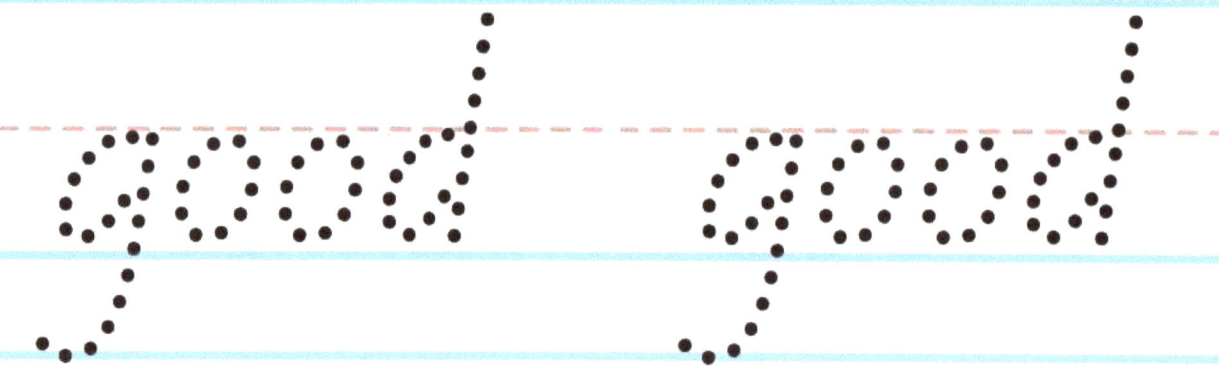

- Fill in the missing letters to write the word.

g_od   goo_

_ood

g_ _d

go_ _   _ _ _d

- Complete the sentence with the missing word.

Ice cream is so ___.

37

green

- Say the word. Then trace the word. Write the word.

green green

- Find and circle the word **this** three times.

G d l k g r e e n
g r e e n o d r h
o n a s t r r b i
s f g r e e n m s

- Complete the sentence with the missing word.

My hat is _____

like

- Say the word. Then trace the word. Write the word.

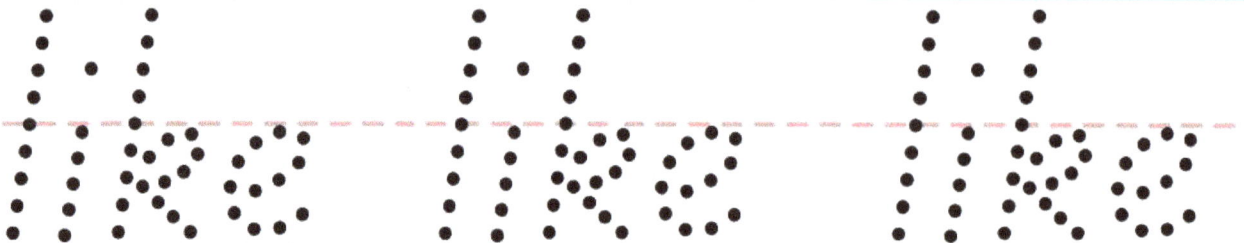

- Color each space that has the word **like**.

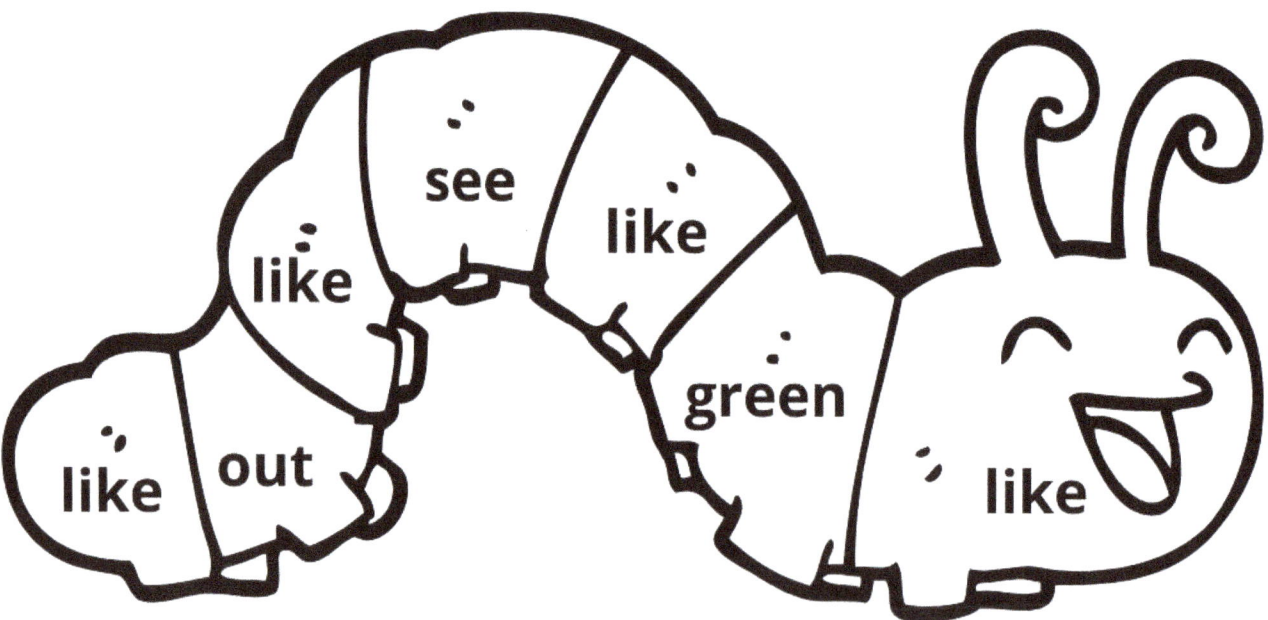

- Complete the sentence with the missing word.

I _____ my kitty.

look

- Say the word. Then trace the word. Write the word.

look look look

- Find the word **look**. Draw a line to connect the letters.

s	h	o	k
l	o	h	e

- Complete the sentence with the missing word.

___ at my sister!

long

- Say the word. Then trace the word. Write the word.

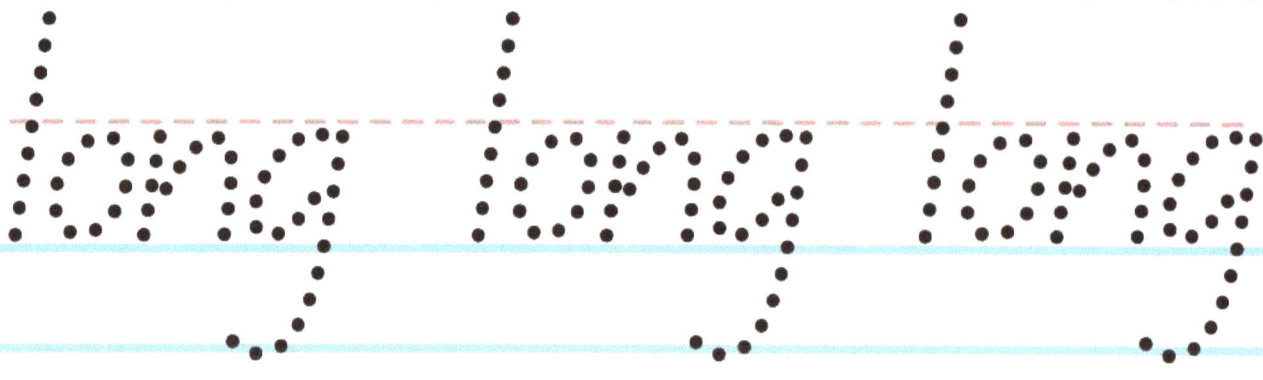

- Circle each mug that has the word **long**.

- Complete the sentence with the missing word.

I have ___ hair.

41

little

- Say the word. Then trace the word. Write the word.

  little   little

- Fill in the missing letters to write the word **little**.

  li_ _le   _ittl_

  _ _tt_ _ _   l_ _ _le

  _ _ _ _ _e   li_ _ _ _

- Complete the sentence with the missing word.

  I see a _____ girl.

he

- Say the word. Then trace the word. Write the word.

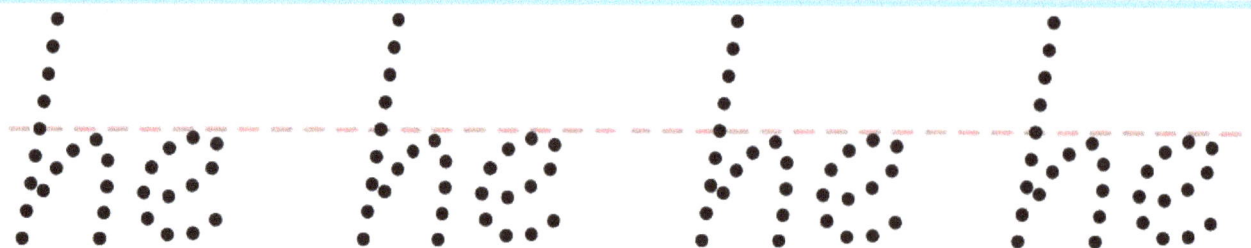

- Color each space that has the word **he**.

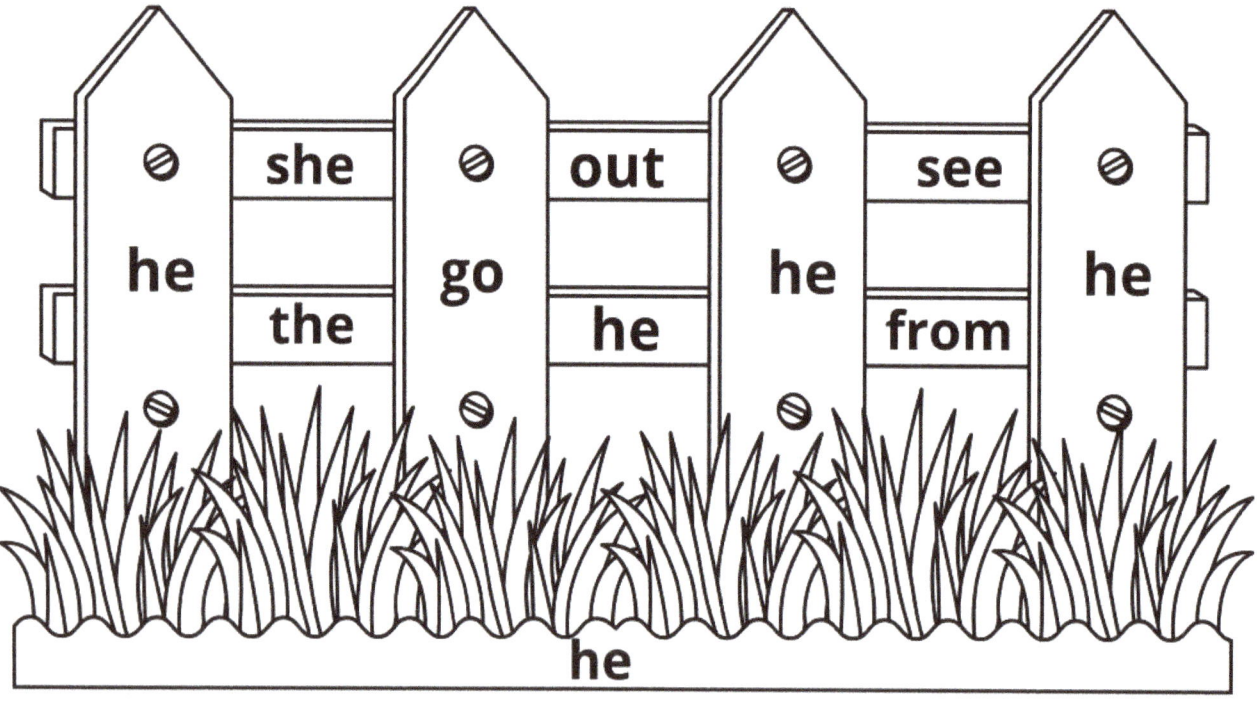

- Complete the sentence with the missing word.

___ likes to run.

- Say the word. Then trace the word. Write the word.

here   here

- Color each cloud that has the word **here**.

- Complete the sentence with the missing word.

My bus is ___.

have

- Say the word. Then trace the word. Write the word.

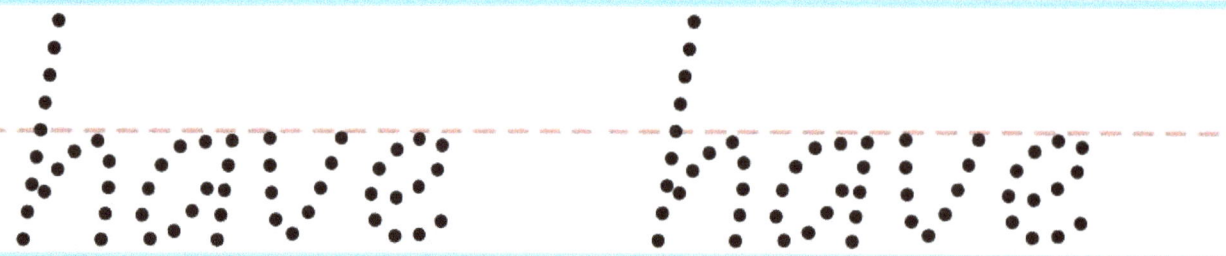

- Find the word **have**. Draw a line to connect the letters.

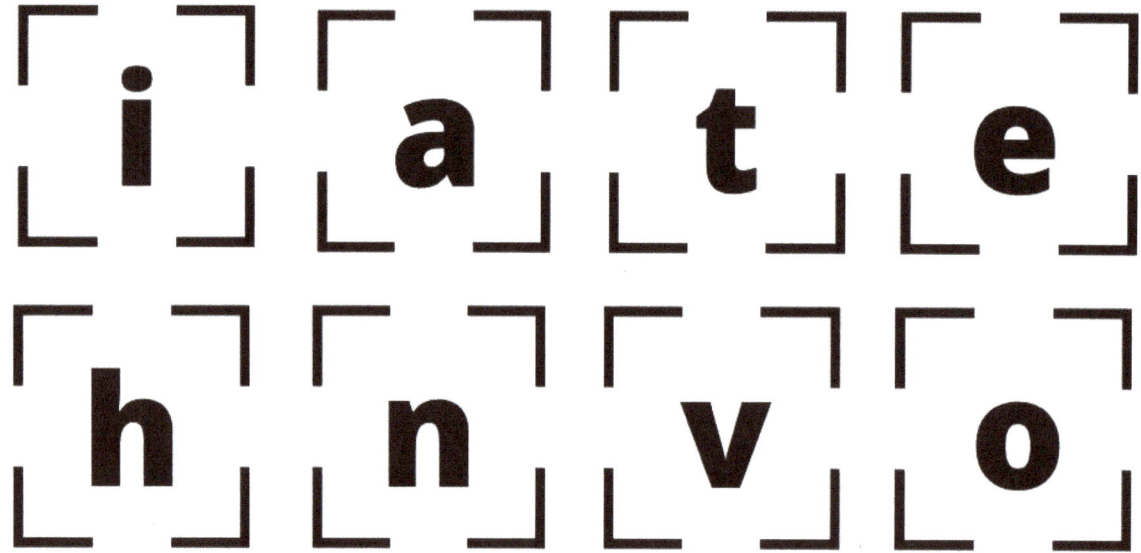

- Complete the sentence with the missing word.

I _____ a fish.

how

- Say the word. Then trace the word. Write the word.

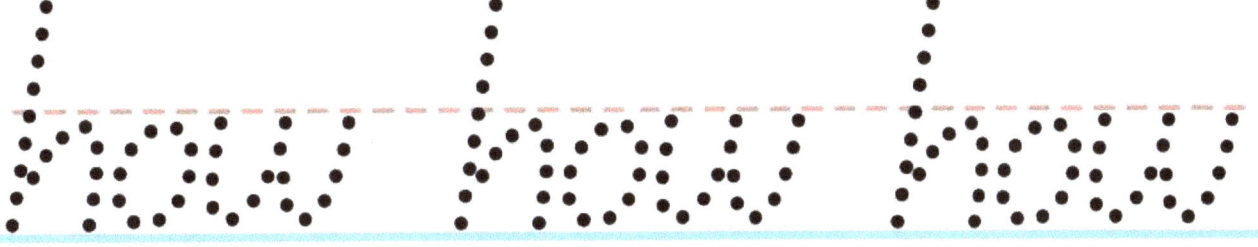

- Circle each fish that has the word **how**.

- Complete the sentence with the missing word.

_____ do you do?

use

- Say the word. Then trace the word. Write the word.

use use use

- Color each space that has the word **use**.

use	find	are	use	over	my
and	two	use	this	use	make
my	use	into	like	all	use

- Complete the sentence with the missing word.

I _____ a fork.

up

- Say the word. Then trace the word. Write the word.

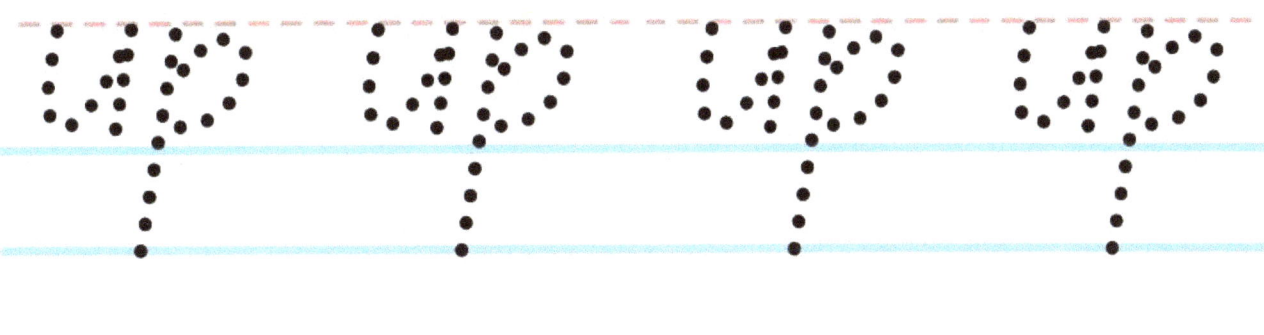

- Color each step that has the word **up**.

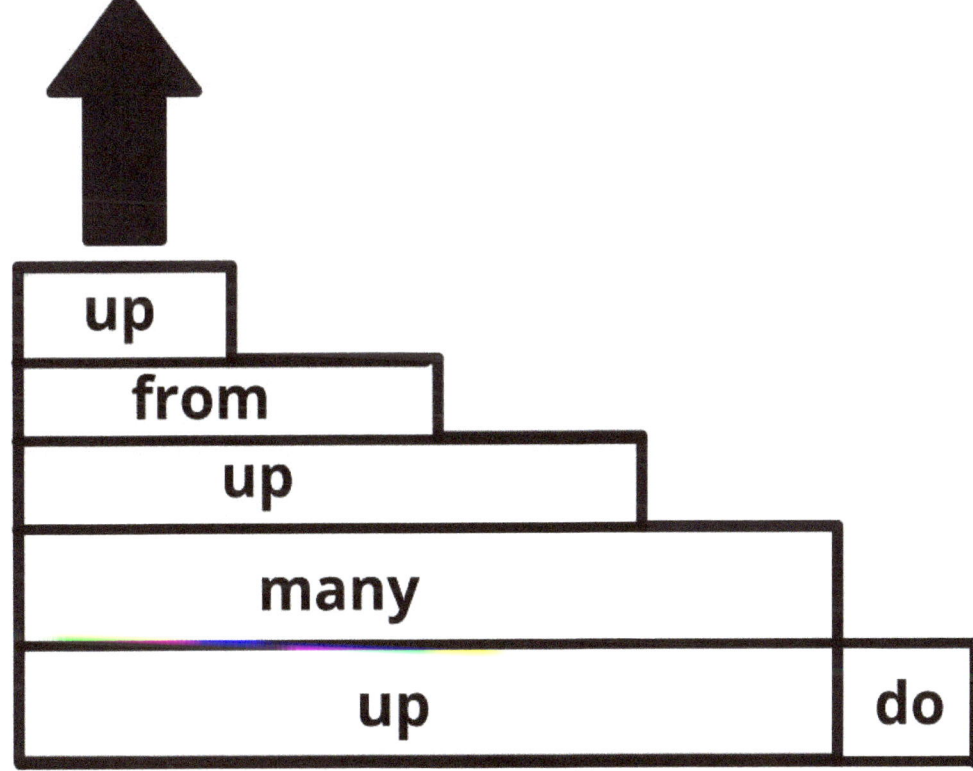

- Complete the sentence with the missing word.

The sun is ___.

can

- Say the word. Then trace the word.

  c a n   c a n   c a n

- Write the word.

- Fill in the missing letters to write the word.

  c_n   ca_   _an

  __n   c__   _a_

- Complete the sentence with the missing word.

  I ___ swim.

- Say the word. Then trace the word.

  come   come

- Write the word.

- Circle each acorn that has the word **come**.

- Complete the sentence with the missing word.

  ___ and play with me.

call

- Say the word. Then trace the word.

  call   call   call

- Write the word.

- Find and circle the word **call** three times.

  c a l l c
  a b c x a
  l n a s l
  l f h i l

- Complete the sentence with the missing word.

I _____ my mom every day.

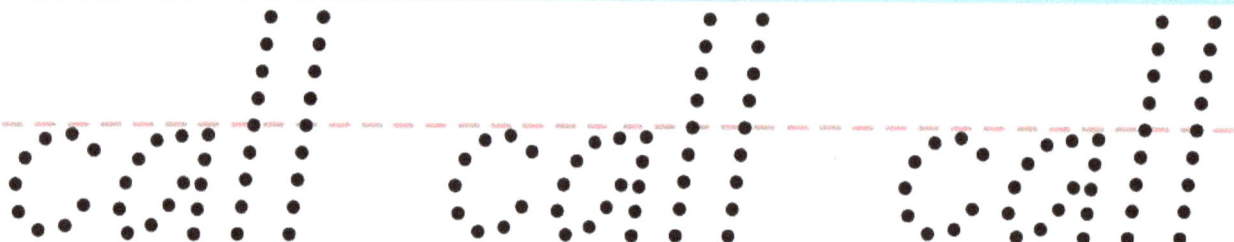

51

could

- Say the word. Then trace the word.

  could   could

- Write the word.

- Color each space that has the word **could**.

  could | here | green | could

  come | could | she | over

- Complete the sentence with the missing word.

We ___ go home.

be

- Say the word. Then trace the word.

  be be be be

- Write the word.

- Color each space that has the word **be**.

my	be	are	be	out	get
as	find	and	be	see	me
be	more	be	all	day	I

- Complete the sentence with the missing word.

I like to ___ good.

53

big

- Say the word. Then trace the word.

  big *big* *big*

- Write the word.

- Fill in the missing letters to write the word.

b__g **bi__**

__ig **_i_**

b__ __ **__ __g**

- Complete the sentence with the missing word.

I like ____ presents.

before

- Say the word. Then trace the word.

before   before

- Write the word.

- Find and circle the word **before** three times.

m d l b e f o r e
o b e f o r e r g
r n a s t r r b a
b e f o r e f m q

- Complete the sentence with the missing word.

I want milk _____ going out.

- Say the word. Then trace the word.

by by by by

- Write the word.

- Circle each apple that has the word **by**.

- Complete the sentence with the missing word.

This was made ___ grandma.

no

- Say the word. Then trace the word. Write the word.

no no no no

- Color each star that has the word **no**.

- Complete the sentence with the missing word.

I see ___ problem.

now

- Say the word. Then trace the word. Write the word.

now now now

- Find the word **now**. Draw a line to connect the letters.

n	d	w	a
w	o	p	m

- Complete the sentence with the missing word.

_____ you see me.

not

- Say the word. Then trace the word. Write the word.

- Fill in the missing letters to write the word.

n_t **_ot** **no_**

_ _t **_o_** **n_ _**

- Complete the sentence with the missing word.

Do ___ enter!

59

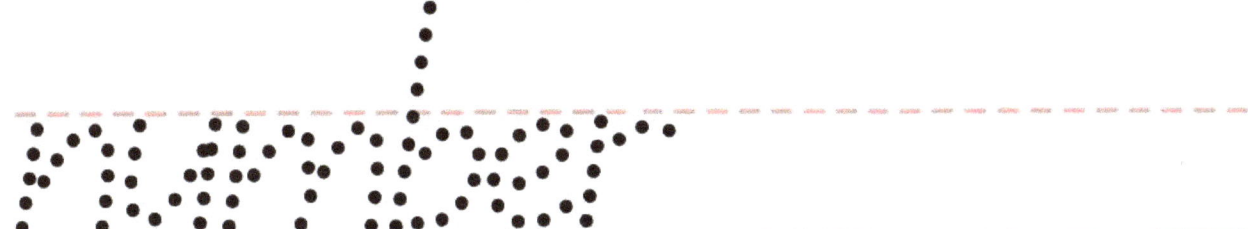

- Say the word. Then trace the word. Write the word.

number

- Find and circle the word **number** three times.

n u m b e r o r t
h t h i s o d r h
i n u m b e r b i
s f h n u m b e r

- Complete the sentence with the missing word.

What _____ is this?

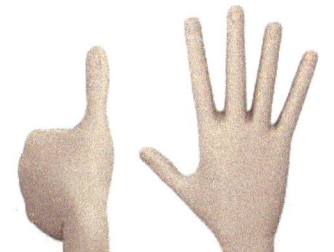

each

- Say the word. Then trace the word. Write the word.

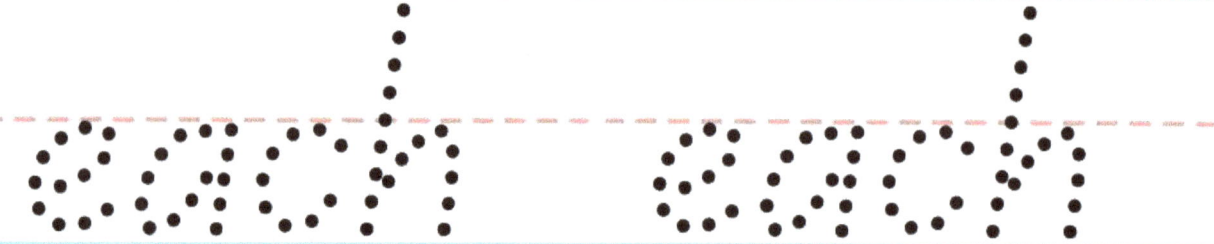

- Color each space that has the word **each**.

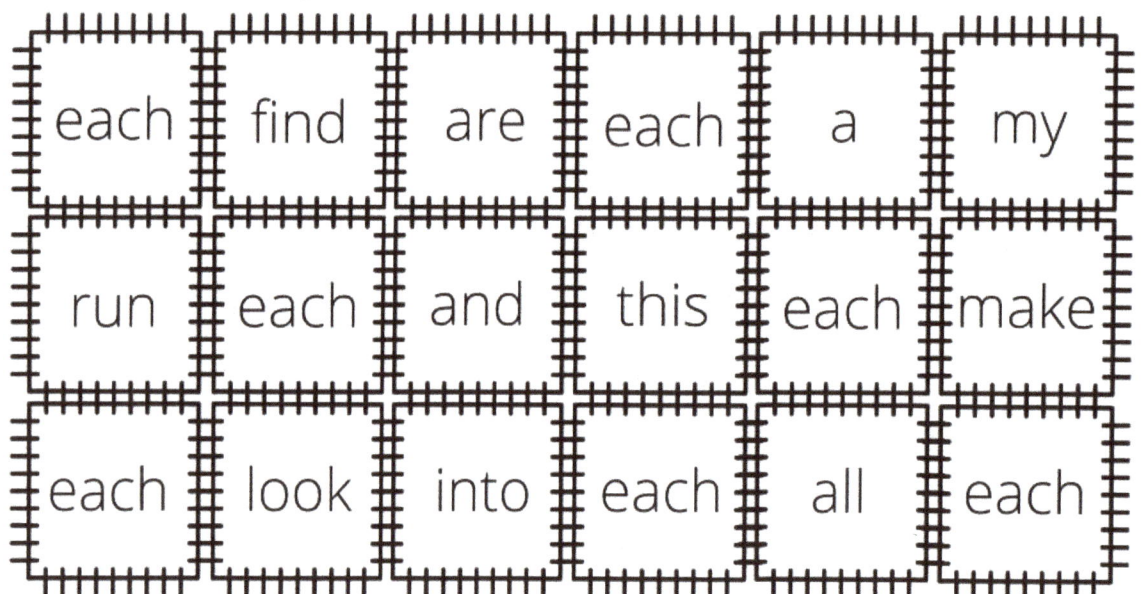

- Complete the sentence with the missing word.

I see _____ letter.

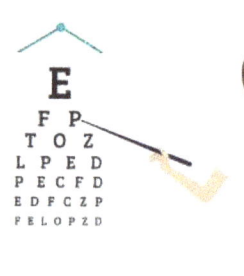

Word search

- Can you find all the sight words in the puzzle bellow?

e	x	b	h	p	f	s	e	e
a	r	e	u	n	r	d	m	e
c	s	z	l	q	o	n	a	y
h	a	v	e	u	m	a	m	i
m	z	l	f	o	c	o	m	e
r	u	n	l	u	i	d	a	y
c	d	z	b	q	o	h	g	z
m	o	r	e	f	s	h	e	f

Word Search

each	day
are	she
more	run
from	have
see	come

write

- Say the word. Then trace the word.

write   write

- Write the word.

- Fill in the missing letters to write the word.

wr_te   _rite   w_ite

_ _ite   wri_ _   w_i_e

- Complete the sentence with the missing word.

I love to _____ letters.

we

- Say the word. Then trace the word.

- Write the word.

- Circle each walnut that has the word **we**.

- Complete the sentence with the missing word.

___ **like to write.**

was

- Say the word. Then trace the word.

was   was   was

- Write the word.

- Find and circle the word **was** three times.

a d w a s
s b c x a
s w a s s
c f w a s

- Complete the sentence with the missing word.

Your brother _____ here.

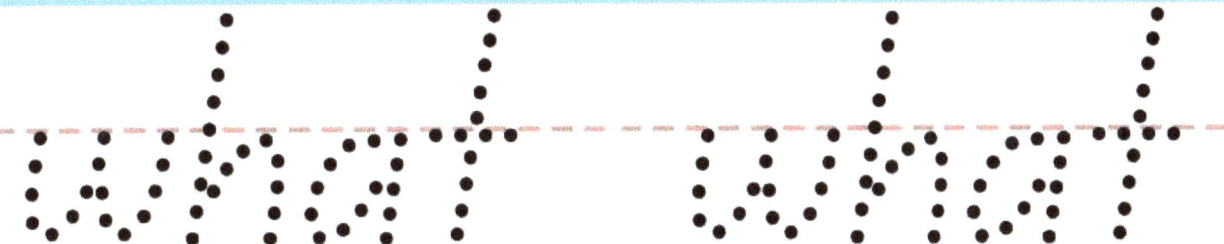

- Say the word. Then trace the word.

  what   what

- Write the word.

- Color each space that has the word **what**.

- Complete the sentence with the missing word.

____ are you doing now?

when

- Say the word. Then trace the word.

  when   when

- Write the word.

- Fill in the missing letters to write the word.

wh_n   _hen   wh_n

__en   wh__   ___n

- Complete the sentence with the missing word.

____ is your birthday?

- Say the word. Then trace the word.

- Write the word.

- Color each space that has the word **word**.

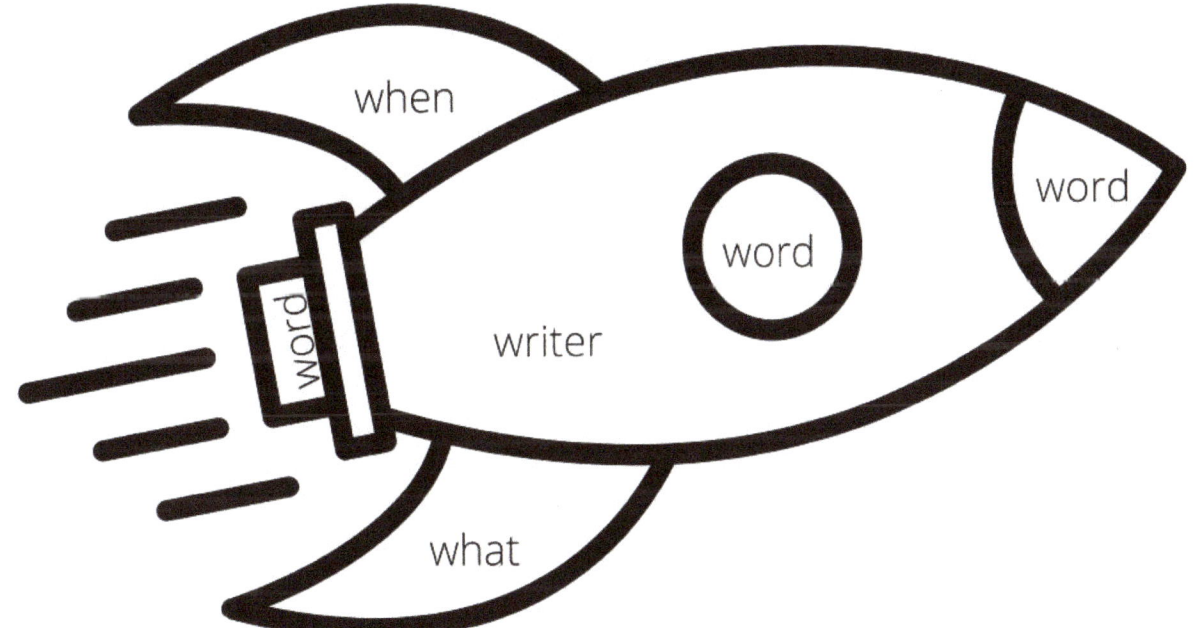

- Complete the sentence with the missing word.

I gave you my ___.

yes

- Say the word. Then trace the word. Write the word.

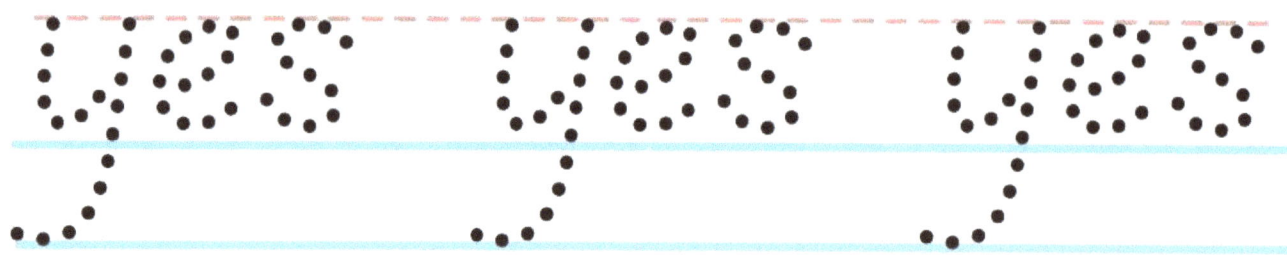

- Color each space that has the word **yes**.

- Complete the sentence with the missing word.

She said _____ !

you

- Say the word. Then trace the word. Write the word.

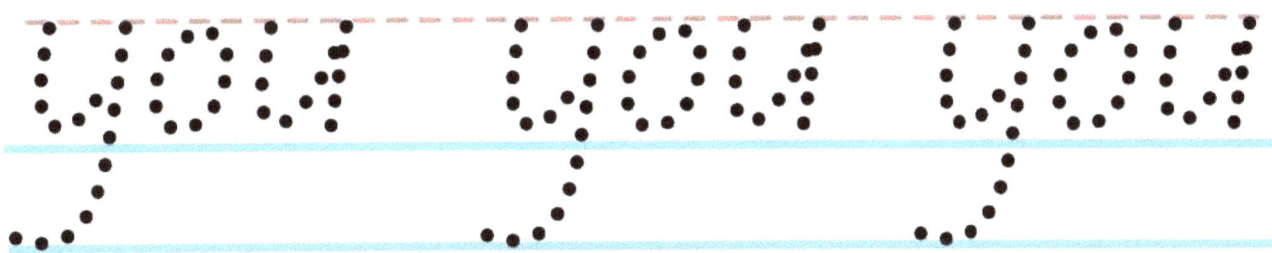

- Find the word **you**. Draw a line to connect the letters.

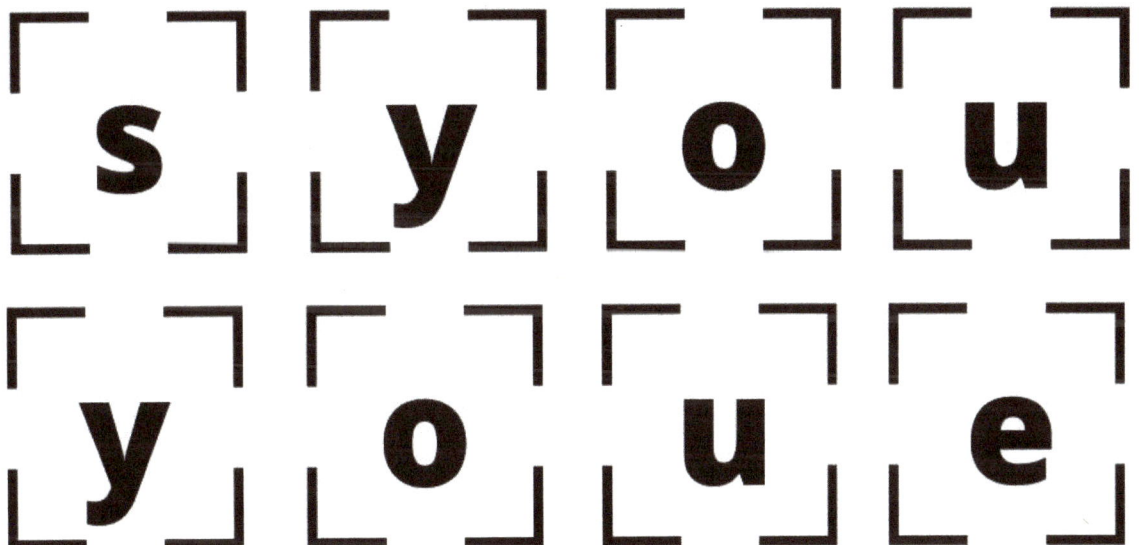

- Complete the sentence with the missing word.

____ are my best friend.

yellow

- Say the word. Then trace the word. Write the word.

- Circle each fish that has the word **yellow**.

- Complete the sentence with the missing word.

My favorite color is _____.

your

- Say the word. Then trace the word. Write the word.

your   your

- Fill in the missing letters to write the word **some**.

you_   _our

yo__r   y___r

_o__r   y_ _ _

- Complete the sentence with the missing word.

I like ___ shoes.

Answer Key

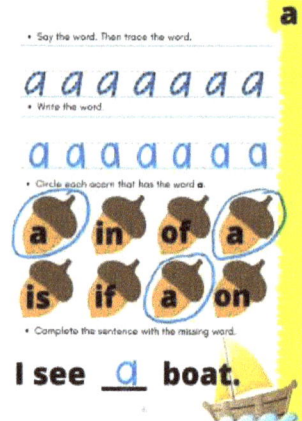

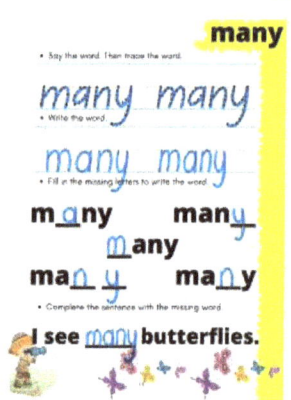

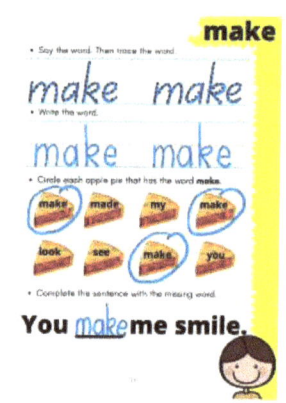

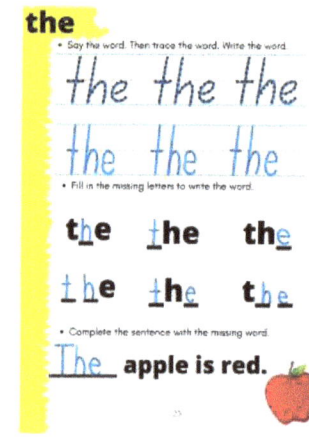
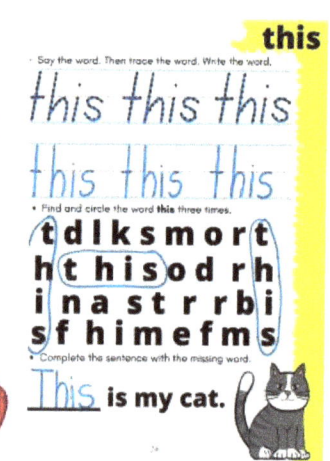

Answer Key

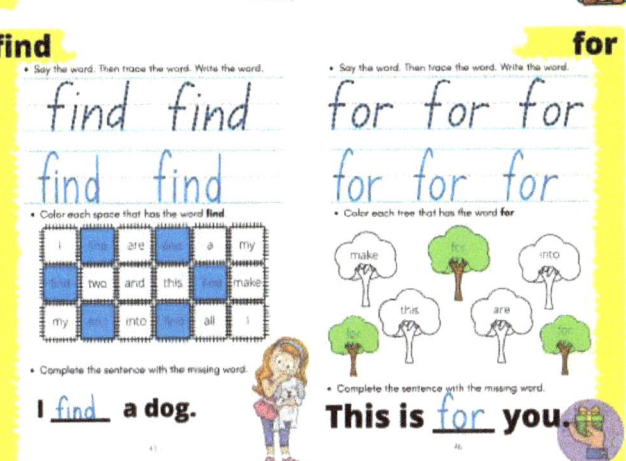

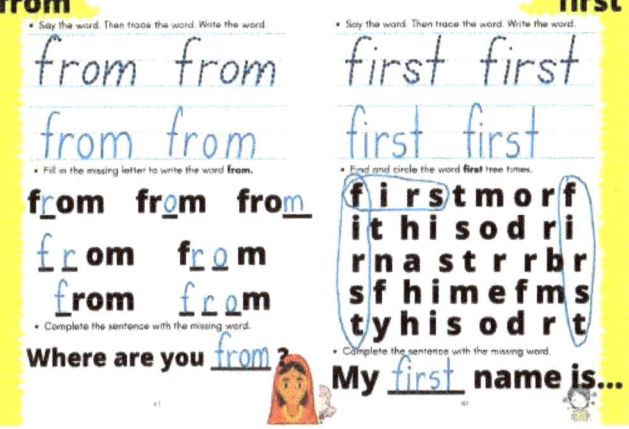

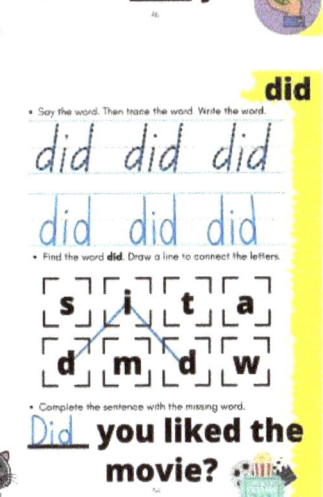

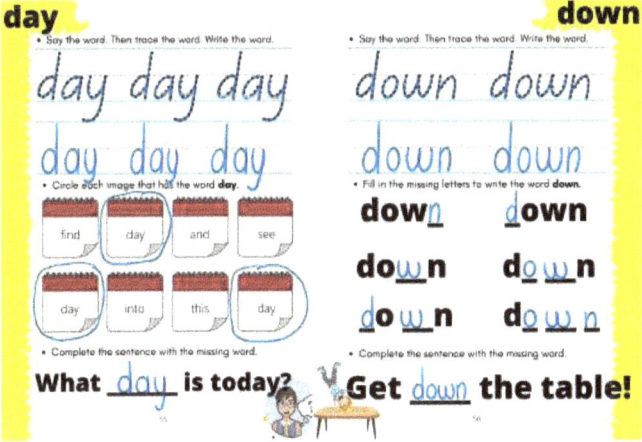

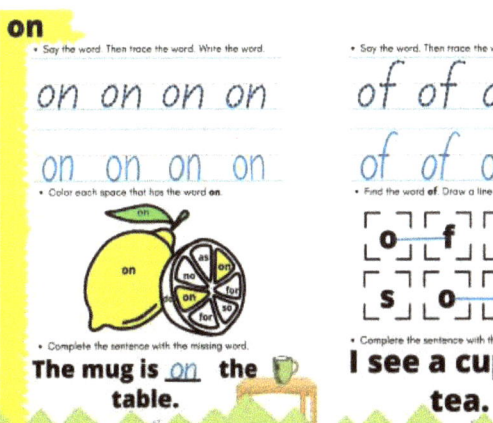

Answer Key

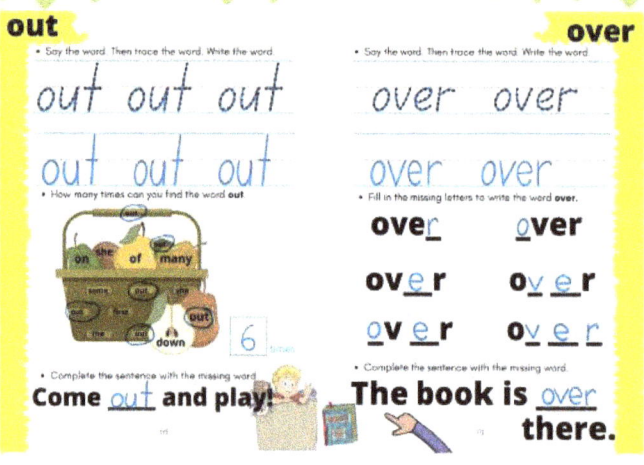

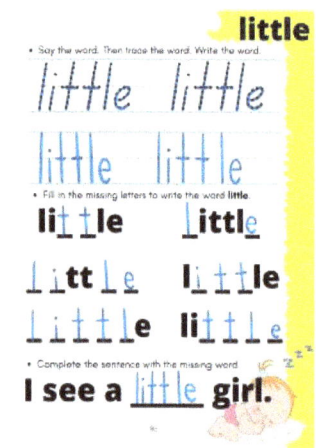

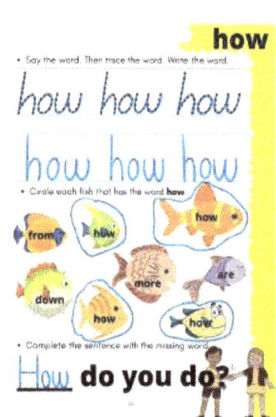

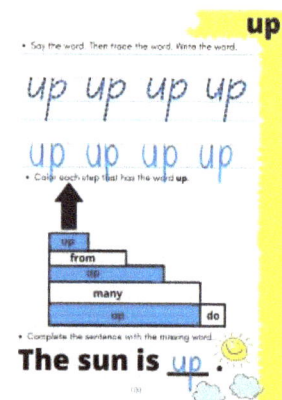

Answer Key

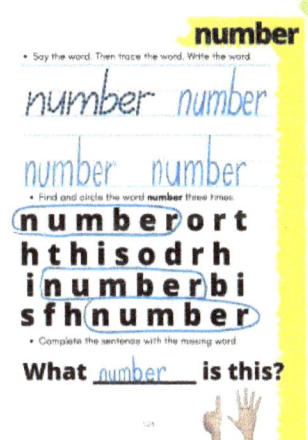
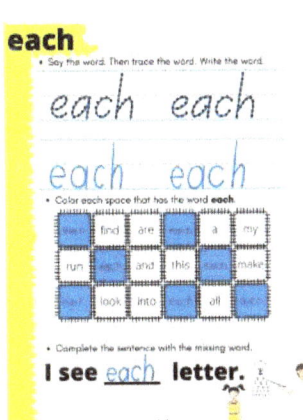

Answer Key

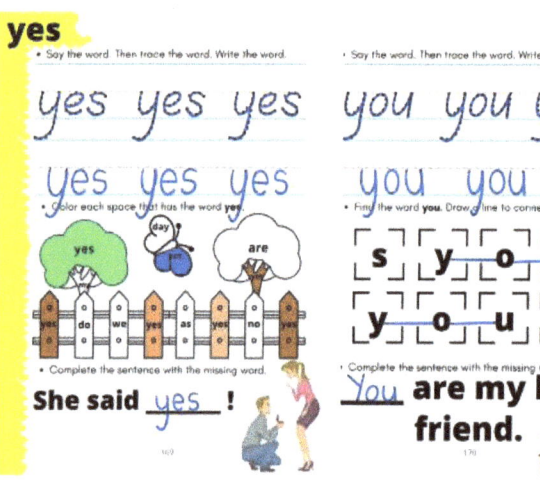

see	she
so	some

can | come
call | could

write | we
was | what

when	word
just	yes

HELLEN M. ANVIL

Join us for a gathering to celebrate a life of continuous learning.

 /helen.anvil

 /helen.anvil

 helen.m.anvil@gmail.com

 Copyrights 2021 - All rights reserved

You may not reproduce, duplicate or send the contents of this book without direct written permission from the author. You cannot hereby despite any circumstance blame the publisher or hold him or her te legal responsibility for any reparation, compensation or monetary forfeiture owing to the information included herein, either in a direct or indirect way.

Legal Notice: This book has copyright protection. You can use the book for personal purpose. You should not sell, use, alter, distribute, quote, take excerpts or paraphrase in part of whole the material contained in this book without obtaining the permission of the author first.

Disclaimer Notice: You must take note that the information in this document is for casual reading and entertainment purpose only. We have made every attempt to provide accurate, up to date and reliable information. We do not express or imply guarantees of any kind. The person who read admit that the writer is not occupied in giving legal, financial, medical or other advice. We put this book content by sourcing various places. Please consult a licensed professional before you try any techniques shown in this book. By going through this document, the book lover comes to an agreement that under no situation is the author accountable for any forfeiture, direct or indirect, which they may incur because of the use of material contained in this document, including, but not limited to, - errors, omissions, or inaccuracies.

Sight Words SuperStar Award

Presented to:

....

For successfully completing all Sight Words activities